GROWAUGRAPHY

This journal is designed as a simple tool to track your cannabis growing experience. Track nutrient use, environmental conditions, and more.

@budaugraphy

ISBN 978-0692861721
First Edition
©2017 Blest Organics

Dedicated to bringing Budunity to the Community

K. Raymond
Founder
Blest Organics

STRAIN	
LIGHTING	ON / OFF
MEDIUM	

WEEK ____ F / V   PH ____

DATE	TIME	TEMP	HUMIDITY

NUTRIENT	DOSAGE

NUTE NOTES

GROWTH NOTES

ROOTS

FANS

FLOWERS

STRESS SIGNS

STRAIN	
LIGHTING	ON / OFF
MEDIUM	
WEEK ____ F / V	PH ____

DATE	TIME	TEMP	HUMIDITY

NUTRIENT	DOSAGE

NUTE NOTES

GROWTH NOTES

ROOTS

FANS

FLOWERS

STRESS SIGNS

STRAIN	
LIGHTING	ON / OFF
MEDIUM	
WEEK ____ F / V	PH ____

DATE	TIME	TEMP	HUMIDITY

NUTRIENT	DOSAGE

NUTE NOTES

GROWTH NOTES

ROOTS

FANS

FLOWERS

STRESS SIGNS

STRAIN	
LIGHTING	ON / OFF
MEDIUM	
WEEK ____ F / V	PH ____

DATE	TIME	TEMP	HUMIDITY

NUTRIENT	DOSAGE

NUTE NOTES

GROWTH NOTES

ROOTS

FANS

FLOWERS

STRESS SIGNS

STRAIN	
LIGHTING	ON / OFF
MEDIUM	
WEEK ____ F / V	PH ____

DATE	TIME	TEMP	HUMIDITY

NUTRIENT	DOSAGE

NUTE NOTES

GROWTH NOTES

ROOTS

FANS

FLOWERS

STRESS SIGNS

STRAIN	
LIGHTING	ON / OFF
MEDIUM	
WEEK ____ F / V	PH ____

DATE	TIME	TEMP	HUMIDITY

NUTRIENT	DOSAGE

NUTE NOTES

GROWTH NOTES

ROOTS

FANS

FLOWERS

STRESS SIGNS

STRAIN	
LIGHTING	ON / OFF
MEDIUM	
WEEK ____ F / V	PH ____

DATE	TIME	TEMP	HUMIDITY

NUTRIENT	DOSAGE

NUTE NOTES

GROWTH NOTES

ROOTS

FANS

FLOWERS

STRESS SIGNS

STRAIN	
LIGHTING	ON / OFF
MEDIUM	
WEEK ____ F / V	PH ____

DATE	TIME	TEMP	HUMIDITY

NUTRIENT	DOSAGE

NUTE NOTES

GROWTH NOTES

ROOTS

FANS

FLOWERS

STRESS SIGNS

STRAIN	
LIGHTING	ON / OFF
MEDIUM	
WEEK _____ F / V	PH _____

DATE	TIME	TEMP	HUMIDITY

NUTRIENT	DOSAGE

NUTE NOTES

GROWTH NOTES

ROOTS

FANS

FLOWERS

STRESS SIGNS

STRAIN	
LIGHTING	ON / OFF
MEDIUM	
WEEK ____ F / V	PH ____

DATE	TIME	TEMP	HUMIDITY

NUTRIENT	DOSAGE

NUTE NOTES

GROWTH NOTES

ROOTS

FANS

FLOWERS

STRESS SIGNS

STRAIN	
LIGHTING	ON / OFF
MEDIUM	
WEEK ____ F / V	PH ____

DATE	TIME	TEMP	HUMIDITY

NUTRIENT	DOSAGE

NUTE NOTES

GROWTH NOTES

ROOTS

FANS

FLOWERS

STRESS SIGNS

STRAIN	
LIGHTING	ON / OFF
MEDIUM	
WEEK ____ F / V	PH ____

DATE	TIME	TEMP	HUMIDITY

NUTRIENT	DOSAGE

NUTE NOTES

GROWTH NOTES

ROOTS

FANS

FLOWERS

STRESS SIGNS

STRAIN	
LIGHTING	ON / OFF
MEDIUM	
WEEK ____ F / V	PH ____

DATE	TIME	TEMP	HUMIDITY

NUTRIENT	DOSAGE

NUTE NOTES

GROWTH NOTES

ROOTS

FANS

FLOWERS

STRESS SIGNS

STRAIN	
LIGHTING	ON / OFF
MEDIUM	
WEEK ____ F / V	PH ____

DATE	TIME	TEMP	HUMIDITY

NUTRIENT	DOSAGE

NUTE NOTES

GROWTH NOTES

ROOTS

FANS

FLOWERS

STRESS SIGNS

STRAIN	
LIGHTING	ON / OFF
MEDIUM	
WEEK ____ F / V	PH ____

DATE	TIME	TEMP	HUMIDITY

NUTRIENT	DOSAGE

NUTE NOTES

GROWTH NOTES

ROOTS

FANS

FLOWERS

STRESS SIGNS

STRAIN	
LIGHTING	ON / OFF
MEDIUM	
WEEK ____ F / V	PH ____

DATE	TIME	TEMP	HUMIDITY

NUTRIENT	DOSAGE

NUTE NOTES

GROWTH NOTES

ROOTS

FANS

FLOWERS

STRESS SIGNS

STRAIN	
LIGHTING	ON / OFF
MEDIUM	
WEEK ____ F / V	PH ____

DATE	TIME	TEMP	HUMIDITY

NUTRIENT	DOSAGE

NUTE NOTES

GROWTH NOTES

ROOTS

FANS

FLOWERS

STRESS SIGNS

STRAIN	
LIGHTING	ON / OFF
MEDIUM	
WEEK ____ F / V	PH ____

DATE	TIME	TEMP	HUMIDITY

NUTRIENT	DOSAGE

NUTE NOTES

GROWTH NOTES

ROOTS

FANS

FLOWERS

STRESS SIGNS

STRAIN	
LIGHTING	O N / O F F
MEDIUM	
WEEK ____ F / V	PH____

DATE	TIME	TEMP	HUMIDITY

NUTRIENT	DOSAGE

NUTE NOTES

GROWTH NOTES

ROOTS

FANS

FLOWERS

STRESS SIGNS

STRAIN	
LIGHTING	ON / OFF
MEDIUM	
WEEK ____ F / V	PH ____

DATE	TIME	TEMP	HUMIDITY

NUTRIENT	DOSAGE

NUTE NOTES

GROWTH NOTES

ROOTS

FANS

FLOWERS

STRESS SIGNS

STRAIN	
LIGHTING	ON / OFF
MEDIUM	
WEEK ___ F / V	PH ___

DATE	TIME	TEMP	HUMIDITY

NUTRIENT	DOSAGE

NUTE NOTES

GROWTH NOTES

ROOTS

FANS

FLOWERS

STRESS SIGNS

STRAIN	
LIGHTING	ON / OFF
MEDIUM	
WEEK ____ F / V	PH ____

DATE	TIME	TEMP	HUMIDITY

NUTRIENT	DOSAGE

NUTE NOTES

GROWTH NOTES

ROOTS

FANS

FLOWERS

STRESS SIGNS

STRAIN	
LIGHTING	ON / OFF
MEDIUM	
WEEK ____ F / V	PH ____

DATE	TIME	TEMP	HUMIDITY

NUTRIENT	DOSAGE

NUTE NOTES

GROWTH NOTES

ROOTS

FANS

FLOWERS

STRESS SIGNS

STRAIN	
LIGHTING	ON / OFF
MEDIUM	
WEEK ____ F / V	PH ____

DATE	TIME	TEMP	HUMIDITY

NUTRIENT	DOSAGE

NUTE NOTES

GROWTH NOTES

ROOTS

FANS

FLOWERS

STRESS SIGNS

STRAIN	
LIGHTING	ON / OFF
MEDIUM	
WEEK _____ F / V	PH _____

DATE	TIME	TEMP	HUMIDITY

NUTRIENT	DOSAGE

NUTE NOTES

GROWTH NOTES

ROOTS

FANS

FLOWERS

STRESS SIGNS

STRAIN	
LIGHTING	ON / OFF
MEDIUM	
WEEK ____ F / V	PH _____

DATE	TIME	TEMP	HUMIDITY

NUTRIENT	DOSAGE

NUTE NOTES

GROWTH NOTES

ROOTS

FANS

FLOWERS

STRESS SIGNS

STRAIN	
LIGHTING	ON / OFF
MEDIUM	
WEEK ____ F / V	PH ____

DATE	TIME	TEMP	HUMIDITY

NUTRIENT	DOSAGE

NUTE NOTES

GROWTH NOTES

ROOTS

FANS

FLOWERS

STRESS SIGNS

STRAIN	
LIGHTING	ON / OFF
MEDIUM	
WEEK ____ F / V	PH ____

DATE	TIME	TEMP	HUMIDITY

NUTRIENT	DOSAGE

NUTE NOTES

GROWTH NOTES

ROOTS

FANS

FLOWERS

STRESS SIGNS

STRAIN	
LIGHTING	ON / OFF
MEDIUM	
WEEK ____ F / V	PH ____

DATE	TIME	TEMP	HUMIDITY

NUTRIENT	DOSAGE

NUTE NOTES

GROWTH NOTES

ROOTS

FANS

FLOWERS

STRESS SIGNS

STRAIN	
LIGHTING	ON / OFF
MEDIUM	
WEEK ____ F / V	PH____

DATE	TIME	TEMP	HUMIDITY

NUTRIENT	DOSAGE

NUTE NOTES

GROWTH NOTES

ROOTS

FANS

FLOWERS

STRESS SIGNS

STRAIN	
LIGHTING	ON / OFF
MEDIUM	
WEEK ____ F / V	PH ____

DATE	TIME	TEMP	HUMIDITY

NUTRIENT	DOSAGE

NUTE NOTES

GROWTH NOTES

ROOTS

FANS

FLOWERS

STRESS SIGNS

STRAIN	
LIGHTING	ON / OFF
MEDIUM	
WEEK ____ F / V	PH ____

DATE	TIME	TEMP	HUMIDITY

NUTRIENT	DOSAGE

NUTE NOTES

GROWTH NOTES

ROOTS

FANS

FLOWERS

STRESS SIGNS

STRAIN	
LIGHTING	ON / OFF
MEDIUM	
WEEK ____ F / V	PH ____

DATE	TIME	TEMP	HUMIDITY

NUTRIENT	DOSAGE

NUTE NOTES

GROWTH NOTES

ROOTS

FANS

FLOWERS

STRESS SIGNS

STRAIN	
LIGHTING	ON / OFF
MEDIUM	
WEEK ____ F / V	PH ____

DATE	TIME	TEMP	HUMIDITY

NUTRIENT	DOSAGE

NUTE NOTES

GROWTH NOTES

ROOTS

FANS

FLOWERS

STRESS SIGNS

STRAIN	
LIGHTING	ON / OFF
MEDIUM	
WEEK ____ F / V	PH ____

DATE	TIME	TEMP	HUMIDITY

NUTRIENT	DOSAGE

NUTE NOTES

GROWTH NOTES

ROOTS

FANS

FLOWERS

STRESS SIGNS

STRAIN	
LIGHTING	ON / OFF
MEDIUM	
WEEK _____ F / V	PH _____

DATE	TIME	TEMP	HUMIDITY

NUTRIENT	DOSAGE

NUTE NOTES

GROWTH NOTES

ROOTS

FANS

FLOWERS

STRESS SIGNS

STRAIN	
LIGHTING	ON / OFF
MEDIUM	
WEEK ____ F / V	PH ____

DATE	TIME	TEMP	HUMIDITY

NUTRIENT	DOSAGE

NUTE NOTES

GROWTH NOTES

ROOTS

FANS

FLOWERS

STRESS SIGNS

STRAIN	
LIGHTING	ON / OFF
MEDIUM	
WEEK ____ F / V	PH ____

DATE	TIME	TEMP	HUMIDITY

NUTRIENT	DOSAGE

NUTE NOTES

GROWTH NOTES

ROOTS

FANS

FLOWERS

STRESS SIGNS

STRAIN	
LIGHTING	O N / O F F
MEDIUM	
WEEK ____ F / V	PH ____

DATE	TIME	TEMP	HUMIDITY

NUTRIENT	DOSAGE

NUTE NOTES

GROWTH NOTES

ROOTS

FANS

FLOWERS

STRESS SIGNS

STRAIN	
LIGHTING	ON / OFF
MEDIUM	
WEEK ____ F / V	PH ____

DATE	TIME	TEMP	HUMIDITY

NUTRIENT	DOSAGE

NUTE NOTES

GROWTH NOTES

ROOTS

FANS

FLOWERS

STRESS SIGNS

STRAIN	
LIGHTING	ON / OFF
MEDIUM	
WEEK ____ F / V	PH ____

DATE	TIME	TEMP	HUMIDITY

NUTRIENT	DOSAGE

NUTE NOTES

GROWTH NOTES

ROOTS

FANS

FLOWERS

STRESS SIGNS

STRAIN	
LIGHTING	ON / OFF
MEDIUM	
WEEK ____ F / V	PH ____

DATE	TIME	TEMP	HUMIDITY

NUTRIENT	DOSAGE

NUTE NOTES

GROWTH NOTES

ROOTS

FANS

FLOWERS

STRESS SIGNS

STRAIN	
LIGHTING	ON / OFF
MEDIUM	
WEEK ____ F / V	PH ____

DATE	TIME	TEMP	HUMIDITY

NUTRIENT	DOSAGE

NUTE NOTES

GROWTH NOTES

ROOTS

FANS

FLOWERS

STRESS SIGNS

STRAIN	
LIGHTING	ON / OFF
MEDIUM	
WEEK ____ F / V	PH ____

DATE	TIME	TEMP	HUMIDITY

NUTRIENT	DOSAGE

NUTE NOTES

GROWTH NOTES

ROOTS

FANS

FLOWERS

STRESS SIGNS

STRAIN	
LIGHTING	ON / OFF
MEDIUM	
WEEK _____ F / V	PH _____

DATE	TIME	TEMP	HUMIDITY

NUTRIENT	DOSAGE

NUTE NOTES

GROWTH NOTES

ROOTS

FANS

FLOWERS

STRESS SIGNS

STRAIN	
LIGHTING	ON / OFF
MEDIUM	
WEEK ____ F / V	PH ____

DATE	TIME	TEMP	HUMIDITY

NUTRIENT	DOSAGE

NUTE NOTES

GROWTH NOTES

ROOTS

FANS

FLOWERS

STRESS SIGNS

STRAIN	
LIGHTING	ON / OFF
MEDIUM	
WEEK ____ F / V	PH ____

DATE	TIME	TEMP	HUMIDITY

NUTRIENT	DOSAGE

NUTE NOTES

GROWTH NOTES

ROOTS

FANS

FLOWERS

STRESS SIGNS

STRAIN	
LIGHTING	ON / OFF
MEDIUM	
WEEK _____ F / V	PH _____

DATE	TIME	TEMP	HUMIDITY

NUTRIENT	DOSAGE

NUTE NOTES

GROWTH NOTES

ROOTS

FANS

FLOWERS

STRESS SIGNS

STRAIN	
LIGHTING	ON / OFF
MEDIUM	
WEEK ____ F / V	PH ____

DATE	TIME	TEMP	HUMIDITY

NUTRIENT	DOSAGE

NUTE NOTES

GROWTH NOTES

ROOTS

FANS

FLOWERS

STRESS SIGNS

STRAIN	
LIGHTING	ON / OFF
MEDIUM	
WEEK ____ F / V	PH ____

DATE	TIME	TEMP	HUMIDITY

NUTRIENT	DOSAGE

NUTE NOTES

GROWTH NOTES

ROOTS

FANS

FLOWERS

STRESS SIGNS

STRAIN	
LIGHTING	ON / OFF
MEDIUM	
WEEK ____ F / V	PH ____

DATE	TIME	TEMP	HUMIDITY

NUTRIENT	DOSAGE

NUTE NOTES

GROWTH NOTES

ROOTS

FANS

FLOWERS

STRESS SIGNS

STRAIN	
LIGHTING	ON / OFF
MEDIUM	
WEEK ____ F / V	PH ____

DATE	TIME	TEMP	HUMIDITY

NUTRIENT	DOSAGE

NUTE NOTES

GROWTH NOTES

ROOTS

FANS

FLOWERS

STRESS SIGNS

www.ingramcontent.com/pod-product-compliance
Lightning Source LLC
Chambersburg PA
CBHW061334040426
42444CB00011B/2923